HIP HOP

Carmel Reilly

Nelson Thornes

First published in 2007 by Cengage Learning Australia
www.cengage.com.au

This edition published in 2008 under the imprint of Nelson Thornes Ltd,
Delta Place, 27 Bath Road, Cheltenham, United Kingdom, GL53 7TH

10 9 8 7 6 5 4 3 2
11 10 09 08

Text © 2007 Cengage Learning Australia Pty Ltd ABN 14058280149
(incorporated in Victoria)

The right of Carmel Reilly to be identified as author of this work has been asserted by him/her in accordance with the Copyright, Designs and Patents Act 1988

All rights reserved. No part of this publication may be reproduced or transmitted in any form or by any means, electronic or mechanical, including photocopy, recording or any information storage and retrieval system, without permission in writing from the publisher or under licence from the Copyright Licensing Agency Limited, of 90 Tottenham Court Road, London W1T 4LP.

Any person who commits any unauthorised act in relation to this publication may be liable to criminal prosecution and civil claims for damages.

Hip Hop
ISBN 978-1-4085-0101-6

Text by Carmel Reilly
Edited by Johanna Rohan
Designed by James Lowe
Series Design by James Lowe
Production Controller Emma Hayes
Photo Research by Michelle Cottrill
Audio recordings by Juliet Hill, Picture Start
Spoken by Matthew King and Abbe Holmes
Printed in China by 1010 Printing International Ltd

Website www.nelsonthornes.com

Acknowledgements
The author and publisher would like to acknowledge permission to reproduce material from the following sources:
Photographs by Alamy/ Stockbyte, p. 18 left; Australian Picture Library/ Corbis Saba/ Marc Asnin/ Corbis/ Jacques M. Chenet, p. 10/ Lynn Goldsmith, pp. 12, 13/ Zefa/ H. Sitton, p. 23 left; Getty Images, p. 20/ Bruno Vincent, p. 21/ Dave M. Bennet, p. 5 bottom/ Frank Micelotta, front cover, pp. 1, 9 bottom/ Frederick M. Brown, p. 4 top/ Hulton Archive, p. 7/ Ray Tamarra, p. 9 top/ Reportage, p. 4 bottom/ Scott Gries, pp. 8, 19 right/ Stone+, p. 19 left/ Taxi, pp. 3, 22, 23 right; Image 100, back cover; Photolibrary.com/ Martha Cooper, pp. 16-17/ Alamy/ Joe Sohm, p. 6/ Suzy Bennet, p. 14/ Superstock, p. 11 bottom; Thomson Learning Australia/ Michelle Cottrill, pp. 5 top, 18 right.

HIP HOP

Carmel Reilly

Contents

Chapter 1	**Hip Hop**	4
Chapter 2	**In the Bronx**	6
Chapter 3	**Rap Music**	8
Chapter 4	**Break Dancing**	12
Chapter 5	**Graffiti Art**	16
Chapter 6	**Hip Hop Today**	20
Glossary and Index		24

Chapter 1

HIP HOP

When most people think of hip hop, they think of:

- rap music

- break dancing

• graffiti art

• DJing.

But, hip hop is also a **culture**.
It has its own way of talking, dressing and thinking about things.

Chapter 2
IN THE BRONX

Hip hop started in the Bronx in New York in the 1970s.
The Bronx is an African-American neighbourhood.

the Bronx

Hip hop started with rap music, but soon **break dancing** and graffiti art became important parts of hip hop culture, too.

Where Is the Bronx?

The Bronx is a neighbourhood in New York, USA.

Chapter 3

RAP MUSIC

In the 1970s, DJs from Jamaica started playing at parties in the Bronx.

These DJs had different ways of playing records from other DJs.

They liked to play parts of a song, and then say things in between.

Jamaican DJ Kool Herc was one of the first hip hop DJs.

DJ Clark Kent

The music in the song was called the **break**.
The spoken part was called **rapping**.

DJ Grandmaster Flash

As rap music started to take off, DJs started to use rapping to talk about all kinds of things.

Big Daddy Kane

The DJs talked about how hard life could be for African-American people and for poor people. They also talked about making the world a better place for everybody.

Chapter 4

BREAK DANCING

When DJs played the breaks in songs, people liked to get up and dance. Some of these dancers started a new dance. It was called break dancing.

Break dancing was very different from any other kind of dancing. Break dancers had to do a lot of very hard moves.

Break dancers took this new dance into other neighbourhoods. They set up a music player and danced on the street. People loved to look at them and gave them money.

Break dancing became very big in many places around the world.

Chapter 5
GRAFFITI ART

Graffiti art is an important part of hip hop culture, too.

Painting on public spaces isn't legal.
But, some people liked graffiti art a lot.
They asked city councils to make it legal
in some places.
The councils said yes, and handed over
some public spaces
for artists to paint on!

People liked graffiti art so much that they started to use it on other things – like on clothes and record covers.

Graffiti art is a big part of hip hop today.

HIP HOP TODAY

It took a long time for hip hop to become popular outside African-American neighbourhoods.

Eminem

Missy Elliot performing in Edinburgh, Scotland

Today DJing, rap music, break dancing and graffiti art are popular all around the world.

But, for people in places like the Bronx, hip hop is about more than just the music and the art.

It's a way for these people to talk to each other and tell the world about their lives, their culture and their ideas.

Glossary

break — the music in a hip hop song where no words are spoken

break dancing — an energetic style of street dancing started by African-Americans in New York in the 1970s

culture — the behaviour and traditions of a group of people

rapping — when the words to a song are spoken rapidly over the music

Index

Big Daddy Kane 10
break dancing 4, 7, 12–15, 21
the Bronx 6–7, 8, 22

DJ Clark Kent 9
DJ Grandmaster Flash 9
DJ Kool Herc 8

Eminem 20

graffiti art 5, 7, 16–19, 21

Missy Elliot 21

rap music 4, 7, 8–11, 21